Drawing
Art for Beginners

Drawing Patterns and Shapes!

The Ultimate Guide to Get Inspired and Create Drawing Art!

Table of Contents

Introduction

Are you looking for a simple relaxing technique that is easy to learn and fun to practice? Learning how to draw is the answer to this pertinent question, and, you are at the right place to know about it.

What's drawing art? Summing up drawing would be a challenge, particularly because people have been drawing for centuries – since the very first drawings appeared within caves. A brief description however would state that drawing involves the use of lines and curves to create an image. It can be done on paper, and many find that it has a meditative effect of the mind. It improves your concentration, brings out your latent creativity, and relaxes you completely.

What's the meaning of a Drawing? It's meditation, and it's seemingly a complex one. But it's very easy to learn, and it's a great fun to practice.

What's required to learn it? You don't need much equipment to lean this unique art form nor does it demand rigorous practice to master it. Moreover, it doesn't take much time to learn the basics of the art. What is required is a healthy does of enthusiasm to get started.

What are the benefits that you can get by learning this art? There are many, but I share only a few here. Like meditation, it relaxes your mind, brings out the latent creativity in you, improves your concentration, and brings you peace of mind. It also teaches you the value of patience and beauty.

Are there any additional benefits? Yes. It's an excellent pastime for some, a creative art for some other people, therapy for a few who are in the process of recovery and an outlet that allows for self-expression. It boosts your self-confidence and raises your self-esteem.

Through the chapters of this book, you will learn all about the creative aspects of drawing, and get the latest tips on how you can become a fantastic budding artist.

Chapter 1:
What's Drawing Method of Art?

Drawing is a simple art form of drawing patterns following some simple principles. The founders of the art have prescribed certain simple rules to draw for keeping it unique and simple.

The best way that one can start drawing is by learning how to doodle. This is a technique that is often taught to children, but even in adults, it brings out creativity, and encourages the development of artistic passion. Usually, doodles are drawn on a 3.5-inch square white sheet of paper called tiles. You need to have fine pencils and fine pointed black pens to draw patterns on the tiles. Doodling is an art using dark lines drawn in complex and mystifying patterns on white paper. To put it in a simpler form, it is just drawing designs on paper. But there is a method and some simple principles prescribed to get the rich benefits it offers.

The main intent of the founders of doodling was to keep the art as simple as possible. Simplicity is the cornerstone of this particular art. It is a basic principle of drawing art. You don't need to buy any special equipment to practice it. Moreover, you don't need to be an artist to learn this particular art. Anybody can learn it and it is open to all. This particular special feature of the art is attracting thousands of followers to the doodling method of art.

The art piece is drawn on small squares of fine white paper with no particular orientation. That is you can start from any side, and you can look at from any angle. There are no rules for what you should draw on the tiles. But to keep it simple and to make a beginning, a few guidelines are given. With no particular design in the mind, you start drawing the curves and go on repeating the same in such a way that your mind is totally at it when you are drawing the art.

The one thing it requires most is your attention. Once you have drawn the outlines, you need to mentally be there when you are drawing the intricate patterns. When you draw the curves one after another repeatedly, a pattern emerges to your great surprise. You will be amazed at the intricacy and artistry in the doodle you have just created. This is an exercise of mindfulness.

If you are wondering how this particular art form was conceived, you must know the origin of this Drawing art and how the founders of the art accidentally experienced the calming effect of the activity before they developed this further into a practice of art.

The founders of the art of this type of Drawing, Maria and her husband Rich described how they came across the idea of developing the art when they wanted to create the same experience of peace and joy for all which they had experienced.

When Maria described her experience of drawing background patterns on a manuscript, she expressed her feelings of timelessness, freedom and well-being and complete focus on what she was doing.

To her husband Rich, Maria's descriptive words of her experience perfectly sounded like the effect of meditation. Awe-struck by her experience, they hit upon the idea of creating a simple art that is funny and easy-to-learn.

Types of drawing as a method of art

Drawings are classified into different types, and each type is unique in its own sense. The choice you make will depend on the challenges that you want to uncover along the way.

a) Portraits: portraits are drawings of people, with particular emphasis on the subject's face and the facial expressions so as to capture the emotions and personality of that person. These are very important in a drawing, and so an artist must be able to depict them. An easier way to draw a portrait is in the presence of your subject. This is the only way you will be able to capture the right emotions and personality as well as the value of the drawing.

b) Illustrations: these are drawing explanations from imaginations of the things you have seen in books or in newspapers. Illustrative drawings serve both aesthetic and functional purposes. They are pure visualizations, and an artist is required to bring out the image in such a way that anyone can interpret it the way it should.

c) Landscapes: these represent different types of natural scenic settings although many artists these days prefer to draw the urban settings under this category. You need a wider drawing surface for this kind of drawing so as to bring out the landscape perfectly, not forgetting all its outdoor aesthetic elements.

d) Caricatures: these are drawings that depict exaggerations of a chosen object, maybe a person or a given situation. They always carry a certain message, for instance, cartoons. Some of these drawings can be very humorous, and an artist can enjoy so much fun from this type of drawing.

Chapter 2:
How to learn Drawing?

Have the Simple Drawing Kit

Learning the art of Drawing is very simple and doesn't require much equipment or too many tools. If you can spend a few dollars, you can obtain the Drawing kit online. It takes a few minutes of simple search online to obtain the tools of drawing art.

You need white 3.5-inch squares of fine quality paper and fine pencils and pens. This is simple and basic drawing requirement. Surprisingly, you don't need to get an eraser as there is no room for erasing the lines once you draw. You would have to draw over them. But you need a fine sharpener to keep the pencils sharp.

Feel the Joy of Learning it on Your Own

To have a glimpse of how to draw a Drawing watch a few videos on YouTube and will get an idea of how to go about it. There are many interesting videos that guide you step by step. You need not worry much about how to start drawing the curves. Learning how to draw can be a fun and exhilarating experience. Within a few minutes, you will realize how funny and simple it is to draw a few curves repeatedly following one another.

Find a suitable place to sit and carry the simple Drawing kit with you. Keep your mind focused on what you are drawing. With no particular design in mind when you begin, you will experience pure joy as you draw each line. There are no restrictions on you, and you are totally free to draw anything you like. You will enjoy perfect freedom and joy with the curve you draw on the paper.

Start with the First Few Steps

Sit at a quiet place wherever you like and keep all the distractions away. Keep your focus on what you are doing and do nothing else. Draw borders along all four sides of the tiles and draw two curves across the square dividing it into four parts. Then start drawing the lines as you like. Keep nothing in mind, no particular design or certain image. It is perfectly okay even if your hands shiver and the curves are disturbed. These are the first few learning steps. Hold the pencil gently and draw lightly.

Allow your hand to take its course and let it be free to draw the lines as it likes. Don't judge your lines and let the flow continue. There is nothing right and nothing wrong in the Drawing method of art. Keep drawing for fifteen minutes at least and you will have a wonderful design before you once you finish it.

Join a Training Class

If you are still unsure of how to draw Drawings, you may to choose to attend a few training classes which are conducted by Certified Drawing Teachers around the world. A few minutes of browsing will enable you to know where to join a class, and you can enroll in a class. Well trained teachers guide you step by step and you will a rich learning experience. Once you complete training, you can enjoy practicing the art.

Keep Practicing

It takes just fifteen to twenty minutes ideally to draw a reasonably good looking Drawing. As you go on practicing, you will realize the rich potential of your latent creative talents and how you can bring them out by practicing more and more.

After drawing the curves, attempt more and more curves in the contours of the curves you have drawn earlier. You will be creating tangles by drawing more number of curves repeatedly. Remember that your focus should be on the line that you are drawing now. Not on the total design you are going to produce at the end.

Keep the focus on the present moment and draw one stroke at a time. When you practice this, you will find harmony with yourself and enjoy peace and bliss while you are drawing Drawings.

How to teach yourself to draw

Learning to draw does not require any kind of magic; this is something you can learn by yourself if you are willing to stay disciplined and also with a lot of practice. Take a sketchbook and pencil with you everywhere you go, you will find it easy to get started with a few sketches and before you know it, you have already mastered the drawing skill.

Learning how to draw is always dependent on the artist. Even with the best trainer, one may not master the required skills on time. But if you are willing to learn, you will do so even on your own.

Some of the things you will need in order to learn how to draw on your own are:

- Pencils

- Drawing paper

- Erasers

- Small sketchbooks

- Mirror

- Charcoal

- Pastels

- Look for a book on drawing technique that will guide you on how to get started with drawing. The local library and the online stores should be the main areas that you will check out for this. Ensure that you are using a book that is meant for beginners to help them get started in drawing.

- Train your eyes to start looking at objects and models around you with the eyes of an artist. This means that when you look at an object, pay attention to its shape, contours, shading, texture and color. Imagine the object in black and white illustration. Always think of lines, spaces and shapes whenever you look at an object or people because these are the elements you will use in drawing.

- Exercise drawing by practicing your hand-eye coordination. Start with a mirror for instance and draw your reflection in the mirror. Sketch out the details that you will see. You can do this as many times as it is necessary. The best way to start drawing is to start by drawing real objects that you can see. As you master the skill, you can draw the things in your imagination.

- Practice drawing with different kinds of medium, for instance, pencils, charcoal and pen, and ink. It is good to master the skill of using all of them, and then you will be able to choose the right one to use for a specific drawing. Try different kinds of shades using a range mediums. This will help you figure out the kind of medium to use for a certain result. As you practice, try out different kinds of drawings and sketches and have fun as well so as to make it easy to experiment more with the mediums.

- You have to practice drawing every day. This may not go so well with beginners who do not have the confidence to draw yet, but look at it as the practice you need in order to master the final skill. If you make drawing a priority in your life, you will have an easy time mastering the required skills and some amazing techniques as well. It will also not be long before you are able to draw like a pro.

- Choose your own style and use it for your drawings. Do not try to copy what another artist does because each artist has his own style of drawing, including you. There are so many styles that you can choose from. If you want to be a great artist, you will do your best to grow your skill in the direction you feel fit for you.

Chapter 3:
What makes Drawing Art Unique?

The doodling a drawing method of art has many features that make it unique. People from any background without any qualifications can enjoy creating these Drawings. Here are some factors that make this technique unique.

Keeps your Intuition at Work

With complete focus and one stroke at a time, it is not based on any preplanned idea or concept. When you begin, there is no logic in the angles and curves that you draw on the paper. You may be surprised at the end to find a unique express of the curves. The repetitive patterns make it beautiful and the unrestricted freedom when you draw them lead to creative expression.

It's the work of the mind when it finds its flow being in the present moment free from the shackles of past and future. It makes you feel free yet focused on the thing you are drawing

Nothing is serious about creating these drawings. This type of drawing requires mindfulness. You will experience joy and peace of mind when you sit in a quiet place and let your mind focus on each stroke you draw. You will say that there can be nothing more relaxing after a few days of practice.

It's like a Ceremonial Experience

Drawing a doodle is a simple ritual to celebrate. You find a suitable place, you keep the right tools, and you keep your mind focused on each stroke you put on the paper. It's like a ceremony. There is a beauty and discipline to it. You cannot violate any of these, yet it offers complete freedom. You have no restrictions for expressing your creativity.

This drawing method of art is a timeless art. It is not influenced by technology and lasts long. In fact, it keeps you free from all the restrictions and conditions that technology puts on your mind. You need not worry about recharging batteries and finding the right cable and plug pin. It frees the mind from all these entanglements and opens it for a rich and unique experience.

It's Timeless and Worth Preserving

A true piece of art is timeless. Its beauty and appeal will be forever. Many things around us keep changing, but a true work of art remains for long preserving the rich human experience. The Drawings you have created will have lasting value as works of art. They are the representations of the true artistic spirit that found expression through them.

Chapter 4:
Does it fit in Modern lifestyle?

Perfectly! Nothing is easier to carry with you than the simple Drawing kit. Wherever you go, you can take it with you as it is light weight and doesn't occupy much space.

What makes a perfect travel companion?

People today prefer light weight gadgets that are easy to carry around while traveling. These gadgets should be portable, handy, make them happy and keep them occupied.

The modern electronic gadgets like the iPhone and iPad are the most preferred ones for many people across the world. But you have to carry along all the power cables for recharge and plan ahead for power backup. Many a time, you end up not finding the power sockets nearby.

Drawing Kits are Portable

What makes the Drawing kit unique is its portability and light weight. You do not need to carry a cumbersome bag with you wherever you go. Moreover, the small pieces of paper and a pen are the simplest things you can carry in your handbags or pockets.

It perfectly matches our modern lifestyle. Drawing is fun and can be done when you are waiting for a flight, or once you are somewhere that you have some precious relaxing moments to yourself.

Expression of Individuality

Individuality needs expression, and it finds its voice in many ways. Some show their uniqueness by the way of their dressing or following the latest and trendy fashions. Some show their individuality and freedom by practicing a unique art.

Instead of killing your time spending hours in front of the Television, you can perfectly engage yourself with drawing. You can start drawing straight away, from the moment you choose to. Moreover, there are no restrictions for you regarding what to draw. As long as you want to draw something, you are free to draw anything.

Chapter 5:
Drawing Techniques Useful for Beginners

Drawing is fun! This is a skill that will bring a lot of great benefits in your life if you master it. There are different types of drawing techniques that a beginner can learn before they can decide on the technique to always use for their drawing. Learning all these techniques will be helpful in unlocking the art in you. The good thing is, all these techniques will give great results that will be satisfying not only to the drawer but to the other people that will see his work.

a) Pencil Drawing Technique

To get started in learning pencil drawing technique, you need to gather a few materials that will help you learn the skills well. You, for instance, need the right type of pencil for this technique. Pencils come in different grades and brands, and these make them different from each other in so many ways. To be on the safe side, it is good to gather a few brands and grades of pencils and test them to see which ones are giving you the results that you are looking for.

Another important material you will need for this method is a good quality sketchbook. Artists should always carry a good sketchbook with them wherever they go since drawing is inspired by nature and what you see most of the time. There are sketchbooks that are small in size and can be carried inside a small bag, and these will inspire you to draw something whenever you free; all you need to do is just pull it out and start sketching.

Outlines and line variety

Begin drawing with a harder pencil to create light outlines. There are mainly two types of outlines in a drawing: the light and the heavy outline. The light outline is critical as it guides the artist in the creation of the basic shape. For this outline, you need to apply less pressure and do it in a slow motion. You are allowed to erase or go over some lines as you draw in order to get the best results at the end.

Here is an example to help you create a drawing using light outlines.

After the light outline is created, you will need the heavy outline. This defines the edges of your drawing. The heavy outline is done by tracing the light outline using more pressure. Do not put so much pressure though, just in case you will need to erase some details if you make a mistake. The final outline will be much heavier and clearer than the lighter one.

Pencils can be used in the creation of different line values and thicknesses. If you need a thick line, for instance, the side of your pencil should give you that. The tip of the pencil is used for the thin lines. These are techniques that you can use when shading and outlining your drawings.

A perfect artist is one who has mastered the art of drawing their outlines very well. Therefore this is an important part of drawing.

Hatching

This is another drawing skill you can master using a pencil. What you do here is to draw small lines close together. This is the skill you will use in order to shade across a drawn object. The artist is required to draw small, tight lines, in one

A workable fixative is always recommended as an artist can always go back to the drawing at a later date to work on it a little more to give it better details.

These fixatives are sold in a spray can, and so they are used by spraying on the artwork.

Learning how to draw using a charcoal

Learning drawing using charcoal is no different from learning how to draw with any other medium. It will not be easy at first but with great practice, you will realize that you can draw something meaningful in minimal time, without making so many mistakes.

Below is an example that you can use to practice with charcoal.

If you have been drawing using a pencil, you realize that drawing using charcoal will be a bit different. Patience will get you there.

There are different varieties of charcoal drawings. They can be loose, or they can be taken to a higher degree of realism depending on how much shading you have put on your drawing. They look more like paintings.

Advantages of using charcoal for drawing

Charcoal can easily be spread, blended and erased due to its characteristics. It can, therefore, be used in so many different ways as per the liking of the artist. This means that an artist is not limited as to the kinds of objects that he can draw. An artist is also able to express himself in so many different ways while drawing and so he can bring out his creativity in the best way possible.

Charcoal can be used on any surface that can accept the mark, so you are not limited to the kinds of drawing surfaces that you can use this technique. The best to use though is one that has a course texture for instance charcoal paper, waterproof papers and pastel papers. Smooth surfaces can also be used, for example, the Bristol board, illustration board, and newsprint.

If you prefer to use a toned surface, make sure that you use both black and white charcoal since the white part will be missing on the surface.

c) Granite Drawing Technique

Granites are close to pencils and so their marks are almost the same. Granites are usually graded as per the value they give to the drawing. The grades range between B and B9. They also come in different thicknesses so as to suit the need for any artist. Thick granites, for instance, are used to make energetic marks on medium to large scale drawings. You will need an eraser in order to expand the marks that have been made by a granite.

Beginners may not know the right kind of granite to use for an individual drawing. Again, experiment as much as you want and go for what works best for you as an artist. The good thing with drawing is that there is no wrong or right as long as the image on the drawing is clear and of top quality.

d) Pen and Ink Drawing Technique

Pen and ink drawing technique sounds permanent and scary and so, a beginner artist may not be so enthusiastic to try it out. The fact is that there is no need for you to be scared. There are so many ways that you can use in order to control your drawing using this medium. The good thing about pen and ink drawing is that you can quickly bring emotion and add subtle details to your drawings.

There are different pen and ink drawing skills you must master though for you to effectively use and enjoy this technique.

The materials you need

These are the materials that you will need for pen and ink drawing:

- A drawing paper

- Nibs in a pen holder

- Black ink

- Archival ink pens

- A brush

The kind of material you will use for this drawing technique will determine the line quality and the overall look of your artwork. It will also determine if you will have an easy time drawing or not. A nib and nib holder, for instance, is useful for drawing lines of different weight. There are different nibs you will use for different lines. A brush, on the other hand, will be helpful if you want to cover a larger surface area whenever you are giving your drawing fine details. An artist will pick out different material depending on what they want to achieve.

Some of the skills you will need to learn in this drawing technique are

Linear hatching

This is the most fundamental pen and ink drawing skill you should learn. Draw several straight lines in order to create volume and shading. To have different effects, space out the lines or thicken them a bit and see the results. For a dark effect, lines that are close together will give you better results.

Here is an example of a cat that you can use to practice.

Cross-hatching

This starts more like linear hatching only that you have to cross the created lines with lines in the opposite direction. The lines should intersect and form small crosses, and they should be of the same thickness and space.

Here is a workable example.

Ink wash

This is an impressive skill of the pen and ink drawing technique. Instead of using your pen, you use the brush to fill out the areas of your desire with ink. The lightest wash is applied at the beginning. This is an ink that has been diluted using water. Add more and more value ink gradually on the object in order to bring out dimensionality to your drawing.

Here is an example of the in wash technique.

Cross contour

This is the best skill to learn if you want to bring out the form in your drawing. What you do here is to follow the shape of the object to fill out its shape using lines that flow as per the shape of the object. The way that you shade depends on the kind of effect you want to have in your drawing.

Practice cross contouring on a circle as follows.

Splatter skill

This is a skill that will provide much fun but if you are not careful, it can be very messy. This is done by dropping ink on the drawing surface in a particular style or manner. You could use your brush or nib for this, and use a pencil to tap the inked material in order to let the ink drop. You can use different ink washes (diluted ink and undiluted ink) or different colors of ink here so as to give it a unique look and feel. You can also make it as beautiful as you want it to look.

This is a skill that will make an artist feel free and a little crazy. Beginners can experiment as much as they want in order to give the drawing a different look. With time, you will be able to know what to do, the kind of washes to use and ink colors to go for in order to have a certain type of artwork that will impress not only you as the artist but also other people that will see your drawing.

Stippling skill

This is not an easy skill, but the results are always surprising. If you want to have a neat effect on your building, this is a skill to use although you will need so much patience to get it done in the end. A series of dots should be created, closely together in order to create a form. If you want the object darker, ensure that the dots are very close to each other. Space them a bit if you want a lighter effect on your drawing. Large dots will give a different effect as compared to smaller lighter dots. Work on the surface randomly if you want to create a better visual effect.

Below is an example that you can try from a seascape.

These different ink and pen drawing skills are great if you master them so well. You can combine them in a certain drawing so as to bring different kinds of effects and also to bring out the artist in you.

e) Shading Technique

The illusion of depth in drawing is created using shading. This is also what is called three-dimensional reality. The value or tone of your drawing will be brought out by different kinds of shades. There is a broad range of values that an artist can use on his drawings, and this will mainly depend on how much they can shade.

Shading is easy, but it is a skill that should be used with caution in order to bring out the kind of effect you want on a certain drawing.

There are different ways an artist can shade and these are:

- Hatching

- Crosshatching

- Squirkling

- Hatching involves a set of straight or curved lines that have been drawn close together in order to bring out value. The lines could be far apart or very close together, thin or thick depending on the shading effects that you want to achieve. For a solid effect, for instance, the shading much be done very closely, with little or no space in between the lines.

- Crosshatching, on the other hand, is just like I have explained in the other drawing techniques. The shading lines cross over each other, or a set of shading lines overlaps another set. Again, the artist can space them to his desire in order to bring out different effects. For a solid effect, for instance, the overlapping lines will leave minimal or close to no space between them.

- Squirkling is attained when you cross scribbles and squiggles with circles. This is a very enjoyable shading technique. Artists can choose to have spaces in between the squirkle sets or not depending on the effect he wants to achieve. You can have a very highly textured or smooth shade this way.

Simple shapes below have a three dimensional quality after shading.

Below are some of the shading tips you can employ to make things easier and more fun for you:

i. Hatching is much easier for any artists. This is because it involves only one set of lines. It is the best skill to use whenever you want to draw straight or wavy hair.

ii. Crosshatching is not so hard as well, and it is the best skill to use whenever you want to bring out the smooth transition of values. It is the best skill to apply whenever you are drawing the human skin.

iii. Squirkling is an amazing and fun skill to use. It is best used whenever an artist is drawing curly hair or fuzzy fabric.

iv. Always vary the density of the shading lines as much as you want. This is done by spacing the lines to your preference.

v. You can vary the pressure you apply on your drawing tools as well, for instance, pencil. This will give you thick and light lines depending on what you want

vi. Use different grades of pencils for shading. For light values, the hard pencils are best to use. Soft pencils should be used for heavy or darker values. The different grades of pencils will make things easier for you since you do not need to apply less or more pressure to get different values.

vii. When drawing, switch pencils as the values get darker and apply more pressure whenever necessary. It will be very easy to do this once you have mastered the skill better. Beginners need to know that it will not be very easy at first, which is why drawing should be practiced as much as possible before one can become an expert in it.

Learning all these skills is very important because it is important for artists to know how to shade different values. Expert artists can bring out dark and light values with minimal strain because they have already mastered the shading technique.

As a beginner, you need to try out different drawing tools of different values and see the kind of effect they are bringing out. You can practice the three skills together to see the different effects they bring out.

Shading is fun! Once you know how to apply different values to bring out different effects, you will have a brilliant time as an artist.

Chapter 6:
Sketching

Sketching is an important part of drawing. It involves drawing a rough outline or a rough version of the actual art piece. It can be used to give the artist an idea of how the final art piece will look like. It can also be used to prepare for a larger piece of art.

A beginner can sketch just for fun and later on, they can adopt the skill in order to always prepare for the drawing. This makes the drawing perfect and easy to draw.

Sketching can be easy, and fun if you master it well and this is the right guide to take you through your first sketching lesson.

The basics of sketching

Any form of art will require great quality and the right materials and sketching is no exceptional. To get started with sketching, you need to have the right tools of great quality. These tools are for instance:

H pencils: These are the hardest types of pencils. They are quite useful when drawing thin, straight and non-bendable lines. Have an assortment of these kinds of pencils and see how they produce different values whenever you sketch with them.

B pencils: these are the softest kinds of pencils. They are useful for drawing blurry and smudged lines. They will also quite useful for shading your sketch. The B pencils are the most preferred by many artists and so, you will need a good assortment of these pencils too.

A fine art paper: a regular printer paper can be useful for sketching, but the problem is that these papers are very light and sometimes they are unable to hold the pencil. What you need is a fine art paper, with a good texture, one that will give you an easy time to draw and the results will be great in appearance.

Eraser: this is an essential tool for any artist. You will always make mistakes, and so the need for an eraser is paramount.

With the right materials at hand, you need to make a choice of a subject to sketch. Beginners will find it easier to sketch an image they can see, or a mode, instead of drawing from imagination. You will have to take a good look at the object or model first before you can start sketching.

These are some of the things you need to pay attention to:

- The source of light. This will be a significant determinant of where you will sketch the lightest and where you will sketch the darkest. You, therefore, have to know the direction of the main source of light from where you are drawing.

- The main shapes. All objects are made up of different shapes. To be a perfect artist, you have to know the primary shapes in a certain object that you are drawing. These are the ones you will start to sketch.

Do not draw too heavily. The sketch will be used as a basis for the main drawing therefore you will have to use light strokes and lines that are short. For starters, you will have to erase a few times before you will get the sketch right. You will also be able to experiment different drawing styles for the object before you can finally get the drawing done.

You can try gesture drawing at this stage. This is where you connect the small lines and stroke to bring out the actual object in your drawing. Gesture drawing is best done without looking at the paper. This is used to test the artist's idea of how the form of the object is. This is also useful as it can be used to set the pace for your final drawing. This is the best practice skill for sketching an artist can learn.

Practicing sketching

This is critical, just like any other drawing skill that you need to master. You have to practice as much as possible and see how well you get every day.

You can practice sketching the same object using different types of pencils so as to see how different the shade will be, and then you will know the right pencil to use for a particular shade.

Important tips to use during sketching

- Do not sketch in a hurry. Small, light strokes and lines will give you a perfect and neat sketch that can be used as the base for the final drawing.

- You need to as comfortable as possible since you do not know how long you will need to sketch. A good posture should be maintained at all times to allow you to sketch with ease, without getting tired easily.

- Use a tracing pen, a dark pencil or a dark marker to go over your sketch to make it more real.

- Using thin colored pencils to make light strokes on your sketch will add so much value to it.

- Always have the mental picture of your image right which is why you need to have a good look at the object before you start sketching. The image should come with you while you are sketching.

- You should have putty erasers with you as you may need to erase little spots on your sketch in case you make a mistake.

- Sharp pencils are the behest to use as they always give fine results.

- Ensure that there is enough light in the room. A poorly lit room will make you strain your eyes so much, and this will be uncomfortable for you.

- Practice is what will make you perfect at sketching. Try sketching different kinds of objects that are around you. Go over each sketch in order to add some shade to give it more value.

Sketching is great

Like it has been mentioned earlier, sketching is an important stage in drawing. This is because of various reasons, some of which are explained here:

- It gives the artists the motivation to continue sketching and drawing. Sketching for the first time will not be as perfect as you would want it to be. You will definitely want to sketch again and again, and this is what will help you develop the skill, and the desire to draw as well. One never knows if they can really do it until they sketch a few more objects, therefore this is the right place to start it off.

- Sketching is the best way to learn how to draw. It is rough, fast and can be quite messy. This is the best way to get yourself acquainted with your drawing tools. It will also help you get quick ideas on what you can draw. It is the best way to experiment with drawing, and it can always work in your favor.

- Save so much time when drawing by sketching the image first. Once you have an idea in mind, and you sketch it right, you will find it so easy to draw the final object and polish it up the way that you want. Besides, you want to draw as fast as you can. If the drawing process takes a long time, the end result is always a great disappointment. If you are working on a drawing for a client and he wants a correction done, it is much easier to correct it in a sketch than in the actual drawing.

- Sketching concentrates more on the concepts than on the details, and the actual drawing will concentrate more on the details. This is why you have to sketch an image first before you draw it. If an idea comes up in your mind, you can always bring it up in a sketch, then you can know if you want to draw it for sure or not. Sketching takes just a few seconds therefore you can sketch as much as you want and decide on the sketches to use for the final draft.

- Sketching is for everyone. Artists that want to learn how to draw for instance will benefit so much from sketching. People who are afraid of drawing maybe because they are not confident they can draw well can also go for sketching to gain the required confidence.

- The last and very important reason to sketch is that it is fun. You will have a great time sketching. If you sketch every time you get an idea, you will enjoy it so much. Many people have developed a passion for drawing through sketching. Once you master the skill of sketching well, you will always draw great images that can be enjoyed by a lot of people.

The best way to get started with sketching is incorporating it into your everyday life. Think of something and sketch it out. Try to sketch out some of the objects you come across in your everyday life, or models that you want to draw and see how fun it will be. This will help you so much in your drawing.

Chapter 7:
Improving Your Drawing Speed

As you learn the skills of drawing, you will want to try it out and see how well you can actually draw. The problem is that it will take some time for you to finish your first or second drawing, and this means that it will not be time yet to enjoy seeing your drawing. This can change if only you learn how to draw faster.

Remember that the quality of the drawing much never be compromised when you are drawing faster. It is better to take all the time on one drawing and get it right than to draw so many drawings in a short period of time that are of poor quality. Besides, anyone can draw fast but the most important bit here is to draw faster and still maintain the accuracy of the drawing. It also helps if your drawing looks good.

Below are some tips that will help you draw faster and still draw well:

- When you see an object that you want to draw, look out for its basic shapes and draw them at once. Many people draw the contour lines and the outline first whenever they start to draw. This is still a great way to get started, but it is quite slow. Think of any object in terms of its shape and drawing it will be much faster, easier and quite accurate. However, some complex objects could give you a hard time when determining their shapes. That is why you need to practice as much as possible. With time, you should be able to see the primary shapes of the objects you come across with ease, and then sketch them on the spot.

- Make comparisons and evaluate special relationships that are there if you are drawing from a picture plane. If there is more than one object in the photo, for instance, check out for the spaces in between them, the space between each object from the picture plane and any other space relationship there is. Ensure that you have these in mind as you draw and this will help you draw faster and accurately in the end. Make sure that you have the correct space in mind in order to make the drawing as proportional as the original one.

- Omit some details on your drawing if you want to draw faster. Omitting some details will not compromise the quality of a drawing, therefore if you have to draw faster, it is alright to leave them out. The most important details in a drawing are the values, the lines, and the shapes so other details can be left out, and the drawing will be as great as ever. In most cases, artists make mistakes whenever they concentrate so much on the details as the drawing could end up looking unnatural.

- Use a medium that is suited for speed. Not all mediums can draw faster, therefore, your choice of medium will be different when you want to draw faster. A pastel drawing, for instance, will be faster and easier to use as compared to a colored pencil of the same size. The nature of the medium used will always determine how fast you can draw with it. The colored pencils, for instance, are sharpened in such a manner that they can only cover a small area of the drawing. Using them will be hard to finish the drawing as fast as you would want. Charcoal is also a medium to choose whenever you want to draw faster. It can cover a larger area whenever you are shading as compared to a pencil.

- Involve your entire arm in the drawing. It is very easy to make physical marks on the drawing surface when you use the entire arm instead of just your fingers. Do not draw the way you write. Drawing allows the artists to loosen up and to be easy with his pencil. If you are able to do this, you will always draw faster and accurately. You have to be careful when writing, but this should not happen when drawing. Hold the pencil differently if you want to and freely draw lines and shapes without controlling any muscles on your arms.

Drawing faster will definitely call for knowledge and a lot of practice. It is not easy for a beginner to draw faster but if you are able to draw at least once every day, your speed could improve with time too. What to do is to try and draw several objects bearing these tips in mind and see how faster you will get in no time. Do not forget that drawing is all about quality and accuracy, therefore, these should come before the speed.

Chapter 8:
Drawing and Technology

Technology has affected every aspect of our living. We practically do everything online these days. Artists alike have adopted the advancement in technology to make things easier and better for themselves. There is so much that you can use the technology for as an artist:

Learning

Many expert artists have offered their advice and skills online in order to help beginners get started on the right footing. You can learn how to draw online; there are guides and useful tips that can help you get started with consummate ease. With the internet as a learning tool, you may not need to attend a class in order to learn how to draw. You can also learn about different drawing styles from where you will choose a style to use for all your drawings.

Uploading your drawings

Once you start drawing, you will find it really hard to part from your drawings, even the first and the ugliest of them all. You need to save them well so that you can always have them. Besides, you may need these drawings for your future drawings. The best way to save your drawings these days is by uploading them on the computer.

Artists upload their drawing on the internet every day for various reasons:

- To always have an electronic copy of their drawing just in case the original one gets spoilt or is lost. The backup is really important, and since these drawings will be of great use in the future, you need to have a copy at all times.

- You may upload your drawings on the computer in order to share them easily with your family or friends. The easiest way to share stuff like this these days is through the internet. Social media, for instance, has provided an excellent platform for people to share their art easily and share ideas as well. Electronic copies of your drawings will be much easier to share, and you can get a lot of valuable feedback from the people that you share with.

- Electronic copies can stay with you for as long as you need them. If you are the kind of artist that wants to see your artwork from the time you started to your present time, you need to learn how to upload your drawings on your computer.

All that you need in order to upload your artwork online is a scanner or access to a scanning kiosk.

How to upload

- You need all your drawings together, even the ones you feel are not good enough. Those drawings that have stray marks, stains or those that are torn should not be left out. You can always edit them and correct any damage they might have using an electronic format.

- Scan all your drawings one by one. Scanners always come with user instructions therefore if you have not used one before, you can learn as you do it.

- You can edit your drawings as much as you want after scanning them. Some of the options you get is either to make identical copies or to create a colored version of the drawing. You can also crop up the drawing to suit the need you have at that moment.

- If you cannot access a scanner, you can take a clear and great quality photograph of your drawings using your digital camera, then upload the photos to your computer using a USB cable.

- Once all your drawings have been scanned, save them on your computer's hard drive. These drawings can be accessed anytime that you will want through your computer, and you can share them as much as possible.

Technology is being used by so people all over the world and so, in order to share your drawings with other people, you will have to take advantage of this technology in order to do so successfully. It feels great when you have people to share your mastered skill with. Besides, these are the same people that will help you grow. When they criticize your work, it means that there is some skill that you have not mastered really well.

Drawing Software

Drawing online is a new thing that has been brought about by the latest technology in order to make things easier for technical artists. There are different types of drawing software on the internet to suit various needs of these artists. There are certain functions that the software must fulfill and this is what makes one software different and unique from the other.

These functions are for instance photo manipulation and graphic design.

It is important for an artist to use a specific drawing software for the task it is intended for. Sometimes artists use software for another task and in as much as it can work just fine, you will encounter problems ahead that is why different software has been designed for specific tasks.

There are three basic kinds of drawing software in use today, and these include:

- Victor

This is a mathematically based software. It draws shapes and lines as a mathematical formula. It is responsible for the creation of smooth curves. These curves can be manipulated without necessarily losing its resolution. The vector drawing software is mainly designed for graphic design.

- Bitmap

This is a software that has been designed for photo manipulation and for general drawing. It handles a drawing as a grid and pixels. This is the most common art package that many computer users are familiar with. As artists, you draw an image by changing the color of bits in the map. However, if you change the size of an image, you will lose the quality of the drawing.

- Computer aided design

Computer aided design is a drawing software that is meant to produce technical drawings, plans, and such like designs. This software is mainly used to produce object designs, vehicle designs, building designs and so many others.

This software have almost similar characteristics and functions, but they always excel in their own specialties.

Chapter 9:
What are the benefits?

1) It relaxes you like meditation

Living in the present moments is by far the best way to lead a fulfilling life. The experts of self-help literature have no second opinion on the amazing powers of living in the present moment. It helps you experience the power of being in the 'now'. The drawing way of art helps you immensely to attain the state of living in the present.

The moment you begin to try out drawing, you will become totally engrossed in the process of art, not a speck of any troubling or anxious thoughts anymore. It helped to bring you to appreciate the present moment.

The beauty of Drawing is its unconventional approach. It defies all thinking and planning that generally goes into making of magnificent designs/patterns. In fact, drawing methods proves wrong the age-old principle: starting without a plan is a recipe for disaster!

Mindfulness needs no planning

There is no need to have a distinct plan when you sit down to start to draw. You are about to embark on what can only be described as a creative process. You are bound to see something interesting emerging with each of your strokes following a particular pattern. Once you have completed your creation, you will be wonder-struck knowing that you are the creator of this wonderful design/pattern. After all, it is just the summation of all the focused and mediated strokes that you have done from start to finish.

You could be a novice, but your work of art can still find its place next to a professional's. That is the magic of drawing for sure!

2) It unlocks your Creativity

Drawing frees the mind and lets your creativity out. If some soul searching is to be done, it is likely that many people have a dormant artistic talent within them. By exploring what it means to draw, you can actually unearth your hidden talents. This is a gift that few people can find in a lifetime.

When a person begins to draw, it brings out wonderful opportunities and amazing experiences for many budding artists. In addition, drawing is an affordable way to bring out some excellent self-expression.

Creative people also experience a challenge that could hold them back when they start to draw. The main barrier is self-doubt. Many artists spend years creating art and never showing it to the public because they do not believe it is good enough. They may not trust in their creative ability. When you draw, you can only get better over time. All that it takes is a little practice. You may need a little help to get you started though. If you are not able to find your feet in drawing the strings, there are tiles with a string already drawn on. All you need to do is divide these tiles into four different parts, and begin practicing. This is a guided way to learning how to draw.

Perhaps your initial result may not seem to be an artistic piece in the first place. As long as you take the time to keep practicing, you will become amazed at your level of creativity, and the beautiful pictures that are able to emerge from you.

3) It gives you Peace of mind

There are so many different situations each day that add to the stress that is going through daily life. Many people have a vice that helps them to deal with this. For some it is sport, others entertainment, and for someone who is looking for a creative outlet, drawing can be the perfect solution.

Drawing is exceptionally peaceful as a process. When one is putting together a piece of art, all they need is a quiet place to site, the right tools and the freedom to let their imagination run wild. This is freeing for the mind, as focus moves away from all problems or issues that are being addressed and is redirected to creating a work of art.

The simple movements of the hand, the stroke of a pencil and the chance to add depth through shading and create a masterpiece, represent positive ways that one can associate with peace and drawing.

To have lasting peace, you should make sure that you practice your drawing every single day. You will begin to see the best results when you practice it, and the better that you become, the easier it will be for you to experience longer spells of peace. For sure, it offers a quick way to unwind yourself from the rigors of modern life.

This peace will spill over into other areas of your life, as you begin to have a stress free experience. This will also affect your personality, quite possibly making you a calmer person and addition to your cheerfulness.

It is advisable that you should spend some time drawing Drawings every day. It will have a long term impact on you in resolving your conflicts. You will be cool and controlled after a few minutes of mindfulness brought about by allowing your mind to run free and express all that is within it as you draw. It helps you controlling your rising emotions and keeping you cool, calm and collected. Throwing yourself into drawing will lead to you avoiding other conflicts, and it is evident from Research that avoiding conflict goes a long way in enhancing peacefulness.

Drawing pictures will give you lasting peace and happiness. The pressure may build up in your mind, when you fail to build good relations with people around you. You may undergo many stressful moments whenever you are to deal with them. Whenever you find life becoming very stressful, you can engage yourself with Drawings.

4) It empowers you with Confidence

Drawing is for everyone out there who is looking for an enriching experience for the soul and for self-expression. In a sense, drawing will help you to find yourself. It is simply boundless. It drives away all your barriers, inhibitions and baggage. When one starts to draw, they open the doors up to boundless energy and increased confidence.

Imagine what it feels like to have other people appreciate your self-expression. Picture the relief and joy that you will experience once you have been able to complete your first masterpiece. Understand that the expression of your creativity is the first step on your path to freedom. When you are experiencing feelings of joy and satisfaction, as a result of your efforts on an artistic platform, then you are more likely to build up your confidence as you have empowered yourself.

It is your work that makes you confident and keeps you inspired. The truth is you need not be a creative artist to make yourself inspired. It is the sense of achievement that keeps you going. It is the feeling of accomplishment that drives you to strive for better and better. Excellence has no boundaries. It always keeps you yearn for more for the simple joy of doing that again and again.

Certain experiences are positively empowering and certain others will only make us weaker and broken. Drawing Method is one of the most empowering and enriching experiences you can have. If you can afford a few minutes learning to draw a Drawing, you can perfectly find yourself at peace. So the much desired relaxation is just within everybody's reach.

Remember the great saying 'Our life is what our thoughts make it.' There is always a close inter-connection between our thoughts and actions. When you are drifted by an avalanche of your distressing thoughts, practicing the Drawing method of art is just the right thing to do. It brings you peace and serenity and teaches you how to live in the present moment putting you aside from all your worrying thoughts.

This is what has been the experience of people who have been practicing the Drawing method of art over a period of time.

5) Get a good night's sleep

Unless you have had the misfortune of experiencing insomnia, you may be completely unable to relate to how it can affect every single area of your life. There little denying to the fact that sound sleep is vital for health and well-being. Poor sleep will adversely affect your health and productivity.

Unfortunately, the challenges of modern life have taken a toll on our night's sleep. You find growing number of people struggling to get a good night's sleep for a variety of reasons -

be it night shifts, parties or studying late into the night. If you do not catch enough sleep, it will lead to many health problems in the longer run.

For our brain to function actively, we need to give sufficient rest to it. Remember, you can work effectively only when your brain gets enough rest.

Stop using pills and start drawing Drawings for a good night's sleep.

Drawing has been a great help for many insomniacs around the world. The reason is it offers an excellent outlet for racing thoughts – in effect, it will clear the mind. If you are struggling to get sound sleep, start drawing one or two Drawings. If you do it before you hit the bed it will work miracles for your sleep. It instantly relaxes your mind and relieves you from all the tensions and worries.

You may also think of taking hot bath and taking food may comfortably put you to sleep. However, Drawing has been proven to be more effective for relaxing the mind and for getting sound sleep.

At first, you may tend to feel that it is not working for you as you won't get sleep readily. But if you keep drawing a Drawing before you sleep for a few days, your body gets used to shutting down in the wyay and the mind sends right signals for good sleep.

6) Drawing is a stress reliever

Drawing involves expressing yourself on a piece of paper and you can draw whatever comes through your mind. This is a very easy and effective way to relieve your stress. If something is stressing you, drawing can help you find an outlet that will take your mind off things or help you figure things out, and by the end of it all, you will be feeling much better. It also helps one to develop positive emotions that helps to drive out any form of stress in an individual.

7) Development of Interpersonal skills

Drawing helps a lot with the development of interpersonal skills.

These are skills that will help you with your communication with other people out there, either personally or in a group. It is easier to communicate with other people, to express yourself well and to mingle with different kinds of people as an artist.

8) Drawing imparts one with problem-solving skills

These are very important skills as they help one in life. Just the same way you can come up with the right sketch when you are drawing, you can easily think and come up with quality solutions to some of the issues you are facing in life. This is a skill that is very essential in life therefore beginners have a lot to benefit from drawing.

9) Drawing will help you increase your attention span.

It is not easy to concentrate on one task alone, and this is what makes some people less productive especially in their place of work or in schools. Concentration is important, and this is a skill that drawing will help you develop and maintain. There is so much you can benefit from a developed attention-span.

10) Drawing is a form of psychological therapy

Expressing yourself through drawing can bring great psychological benefits to you. You can, for instance, release some of the tension and stress that you have retained within you from a very long time on that drawing surface. If you are not the kind of person that is able to speak to another person, for instance, a counselor in order to get psychological help, drawing can be of great help to you. Some of your great desires will come out as imaginations that you need to draw and through drawing, you can come to realize how much you have within yourself. It will also be easy to find solutions to some of the issues you are facing in life through such expressions.

Benefits that children get from drawing

Children can benefit so much from drawing.

- Children who are unable to communicate well for instance may find drawing an easier way to express their feelings. If for instance a child is dealing with a traumatic experience and he is unable to express himself, drawing can be used as a means that they can express themselves. Therapists observe what the child is drawing and from that, they can understand what the child is feeling or what they are dealing with.

- Drawing can also be used to build confidence in a child. Issues of low self-esteem, for instance, can be fixed as the child learns how to draw well and express himself on a drawing surface. A child's fears can be expressed in a drawing and this makes it easy for the child to deal with his fears.

- Drawing can also help a child so much in brain development. This is mainly through observation and trying to remember what he saw in detail. As the child comes up with many drawing ideas, his brain grows, and he can think and come up with many solutions in the actual sense. There are so many brain activities involved in drawing and these work to develop the brain of a child.

- Children who draw have the best handwritings. They are able to write more carefully and creatively and so, they end up writing much better than those children who do not draw.

Chapter 10:
Important Tips to Get You Started

Drawing is a skill that can be learned easily. There are expert artists who can draw really well and there are people who have no idea where to get started. The truth is, even the best artists started somewhere. To be an expert, there are a few things you will need and these are: the desire to draw, instruction, time to draw and a lot of practice. These, coupled with a few tips that I have here will help you get started and if you have the desire, you will be the artist you have always desired in no time at all:

i.   Drawing is a skill; it is not an inborn ability that some people have, and others lack. This should tell you that anyone can learn how to draw. You do not possess inherent abilities to draw; you learn the skills and become an expert with practice. If therefore you want to be a casual artist, a real artist or a professional artist, the choice is yours to make as you can be anyone that you want to be.

ii.   Take advantage of any available resource to develop your drawing skill. It will be boring if you will draw just what you encounter every day. Sometimes you will want to draw an animal for instance, and maybe you cannot see it in person in order to draw it well. Pictures and photos can be of great help in this. There are so many resources out there that can help a beginner learn and grow their skill.

iii. Drawing is mainly inspired by observation. What you see is what you will be inspired to draw. Great artists take the time to study the object of interest then they are able to draw it well. You can draw out of imagination but sometimes what you imagine may not come out well like what you have seen. Take half the time to study the object and the rest of the time to draw it. This is what will make your drawing great.

iv. Always look for basic shapes that make up the object of your interest. Every object is made up of different shapes. In order to draw well and to draw faster, the shape will be the first thing you will go for, and then you can fill it in with outlines and shades.

v. Use the right line quality at all times. The line quality in a drawing means the thickness and the lightness of a line. Line drawings, for instance, will require the use of the best line quality. You have to use thin and thick lines throughout the drawing in order to make it more interesting and to add variety to it.

vi. Great drawings will have a full range of light, which is referred to as the value. In a drawing, there is the light side and the dark side. The artists has to bring this value out so clearly for the drawing to look great. Your drawings should always have a full range of value because this is what makes them stand out from the rest.

vii. Choose one drawing style and stick to it. The way you start a drawing should be the same way that you will finish it. It has to be seen that the same artist is the one that has worked on the entire drawing. This is in order to make your drawing harmonious and unified. Besides, one's style defines him and so, your drawing style should be consistent at all times.

viii. Have fun. Loosen up when drawing. You do not have to be stiff and too careful because this could make you mess up your drawing. Do not draw the way that you write, with your wrist. The best way to draw is by using the entire arm. Be flexible. It is important to ensure that you are as comfortable as possible in order to have an easy time drawing.

ix. Ensure you are familiar with the medium you are using to draw. The kind of medium you will use to draw a certain object should be easy to use. You must know how to use the medium to bring out the different values in your drawing. In the beginning, you can experiment as much as you want so as to understand how different mediums work, and then you will be able to choose the right one for any drawing you will want to draw.

x. The best tip of all is practice. You will learn the drawing skill but if you do not practice the skill, you will not be able to draw well. A practical way of doing this is to always ensure that you have a small sketchbook with you at all times. Whenever you feel like drawing, or an idea comes up in your mind, you will just draw, there and then.

For beginners, try to draw as much as you can. Draw anything that interests you and do not try to be perfect at it.

Whenever you look at an object, imagine how you would draw it. Start looking out for its main shapes, the value, the source of light and how it would appear in your drawing. You can always imagine the kind of medium you would use in that drawing. These are things that artist think about every day and this is what will inspire you to draw.

Chapter 11:
Common Mistakes Beginners Make

When learning how to draw on your own, it might be hard to master the skill right and so you might keep making mistakes. Without someone to guide you or a teacher to help you through the mistakes, you may never develop your drawing skill. Which is why it is good to learn some of the common mistakes artists make as they get started so that you can avoid making the same.

i)   The wrong use of a pencil. Different pencil grades produce different results when one is drawing. Artists are advised to try each of them first so as to know the kind of value they give the drawing. If you use the hard grade pencil to draw, for instance, the results will not be as good as the results from a light grade pencil. The hard grade pencil can be used for the shading. Have a variety of pencil grades with you at all times and always pick out the right one, with the kind of value you want in your drawing.

ii) Using flash photography in drawing. An artist can draw from a photo once in a while but the drawing will not be as good as one drawn from a real model. With an actual model, you can easily see the direction of light, you can turn the model a little bit in order to see the other side and express it in the drawing ad you can have much fun working on your drawing to give it an actual feel,. This will not be possible with a photo, and this explains the downfall of many artists. The person in the photo is just facing you and so, you are not able to get the real value of the model in order to bring it out into the drawing. There are so many actual objects that you can draw in your life; go for them instead of drawing from flashy photography.

iii) The head proportion mistakes. Not many artists are able to draw the head in a proportional state. Sometimes the head is just too big, or the forehead is smaller than it should be. This is as a result of how the artist focuses on the model. Always take note of the proportionality of your drawing and ensure that it is as great looking as the actual object or model.

iv) Incorrect alignment of physical features. An artist will draw a model straight on, just the way he is looking at the model. There is always a high chance of not doing it right, especially with the physical features. But there is a solution to this; sketching. If you sketch the guideline first, you will always be able to put the physical features in the right alignment and ensure that the drawing will be the proportion in the end.

v) Fear of drawing black. This is a common fear among artists. Most of them want to go up to dark great level when shading. But if the value of your drawing requires black, go for it and do not be afraid. Try and put a black paper on that region and see if it will really work, and then give it the shading it deserves. Artists should not limit their creativity. If you let yourself free, you will be amazed at how much you can do. This is the right direction artists need to take.

vi) Use of the wrong drawing paper. Poor quality paper will make your drawing look poor and pale. Some papers are very light, and they are unable to hold the pencil. A thick drawing paper is always the best as it can withstand the pressure of the pencil and at the same time give you time to display different values with your pencil. It is important for an artist to go for the best quality drawing materials, including the paper for amazing results.

vii)   Using pencil lines for hair or grass. This does not always come out right. If you want to bring out the best image of hair or grass, use light pencil strokes that look feathery. These will look great and real. Straight hair and curly hair will be drawn differently therefore apply different drawing techniques to get the best results.

viii) Drawing in a hurry. As an artist, you have to be really patient to give your drawing the best touch for it to come out great. You can never draw in a hurry and get the same results as an artist who has taken enough time to draw. If you want to finish the drawing fast, give it enough time and start by sketching out its shape and outline. Do not be in a hurry to master drawing skills too as a beginner. It takes a lot of patience and practice to get it right.

Chapter 12:
Shapes and Patterns to build an artist

Doodling is the form of drawing, where one allows their hand to wander across the page and create a unique design. It is a form of drawing art that involves drawing designs using structured patterns. The results are a stunning piece of art that is reflective of the artists focus and their mood.

Whereas doodling does not have a technique, there is one when you are using the concept to create a piece of art. The main technique is to draw small blocks and then fill each small block with any pattern that comes to mind.

Here is an example of a pattern to get you started.

By following one step after the other, it becomes easy to create a masterpiece.

There are so many benefits that doodling offers to the artists:

- It enhances intuition

- It is fun

- It is relaxing

- It increases the artist's focus

- It teaches patience

- It leads to inspiration

- It inspires creativity

It is very easy for beginners to get stared when trying to draw. There is no specific set of skills that an artist needs prior to engaging in this kind of art. The materials you will need are just a few as follows:

- Felt tip pen

- Pencil

- Paper

- Basic Patterns

Here is another example of a basic pattern that you can attempt.

How to create a piece of art

You can use doodling to create designs that are built by completing small areas of a given pattern at a time. What you need are a few basic patterns, then you can get as creative as possible. It is okay to come up with your own patterns from your creativity.

Example

Begin by taking a blank page and drawing the basic shape of a square or rectangle. A good size would be three inches all around.

Within the square you will draw a series of lines which are known as strings. These will further divide the square into smaller sections as is evident in the example below.

Now you can choose a section of your choice and begin to fill it in with a repetitive pattern. This is not something that should be done with full calculation and planning. Instead, using an approach that is akin to mindfulness is more appropriate.

You can create patterns that are different in each section. Then shade them in with your preferred colors.

Going to the next level

Once you have mastered the structured art of doodling and adding character as explained above, you are ready to try something a little more abstract. The difference between both lies in the structure, as where the first example is restricted within borders that form a box shape, this example is free. To get things started, one should draw a line that is free form on a blank page.

Next, an object should be drawn. Good examples are feet, hands or a face. Then, using the same technique of division seen in doodling, the object drawn should be divided up into sections. Create a series of shapes and then fill them in.

Choosing a Patterns

There are some sources online where one can get specialized patterns. However, this type of drawing is characterized by freedom, and so there are many sources to get inspiration. These include people, the internet, architecture, fabrics, the living environment and nature.

You can doodle a whole range of objects. In the home, your plant pots, shoes and walls can become works of art with doodling. You can also create greeting cards or photo frames and some colorful and unique bookmarks that make great gifts. Here is an example of an artistic piece using basic patterns.

Discerning shapes

You can find patterns all around you. What you need to be able to do is look at objects with an artist's eye. For example, a simple stack of toilet paper rolls can actually be a pattern with two different types of circles. A bamboo blind is an excellent pattern of straight lines broken up by round circles. A piece of fabric with the tail feather design of a peacock opens up design ideas with circles within circles. The patters are all a matter of perception, and they are all created from shapes. Below are some examples of shapes that you can use.

This is a combination of shapes. There are the oval shapes that create the flower. Round shapes that create detail within the flower. Triangles that make up the border. Then there are the dotted lines and circles that fill in the white spaces.

This triangle shape can be used to create a border.

This picture depicts an oval shape in various sizes that resembles pebbles.

This depiction shows how circles can be used to create a fantastic design.

This is an easy design to create and repeat on any part of your art piece.

The mistake you can make when doodling is to try and imagine how the drawing will look like after it is done; you should not worry about this. Have a look at the patterns provided and get into a meditation mood, then work on it as much as you can. You will be surprised at the results you will get in the end.

Some useful tips to use when doodling

- It is virtually impossible to make a mistake while doodling, so you do not need to worry about using an eraser. Anything that you think is a mistake could be a beginning of an exciting pattern that you can use to create an amazing art piece.

- There are no limits to your imaginations. Experiment as much as you can using different types of pencils and other mediums. Let your mind guide you on this.

- Once you master one skill, move on to another complex doodle pattern and work as much as you can. It will be fun, and your creativity will greatly be rewarded.

Conclusion

Now you must have realized the immense potential of the different methods of drawing in art, you will realize that you have stumbled upon a cure for many of our problems in a simple and funny activity. All it takes to put what you have learned into practice is taking the first step. You can proceed ahead following the steps one by one and enjoy the benefits of Drawing.

Step 1: You have already made the progress of successfully taking the first step, and that is reading a simple and practical book on Drawing as a method of art.

Step 2: Get the Drawing kit by placing an order online. If you don't want to spend any money on this, it is perfectly okay to get the sheets of paper ready by yourself. Cut the paper into the 3.5-inch squares and get a fine quality pen.

Step 3: Watch a few videos on how to doodle, sketch and draw to make a beginning on your own. Keep a small note book and take notes if you like. Read the second chapter in the book again before you actually start it.

Step 4: Find a quiet place where you are not disturbed. Keep the kit with you and start drawing the borders first and diagonal curves next and then proceed ahead and fill in your Drawings. Be sure to draw one stroke at a time and don't plan the design before you start. Feel the freedom of doodling.

Step 5: Practice drawing doodles whenever you feel like drawing. Keep all of them at one place to have a collection of your work. Looking at them occasionally will lead you to greater practice.

It's time for you to act and reap the rich benefits of Drawing.

If you enjoyed this book, please be kind and leave a review for this book on Amazon.

Good luck and happy Drawing!

I Can Sew!

Sewing for Beginners

How to sew step by step guide that will teach you sewing right now!

Table of Contents

Introduction

Sewing has become a worldwide art, where millions of customers and individual consumers are served each day, with different kind of products, using the sewing techniques. Sewing is no more a manual and traditional task. It has become a complete digital and computerized technique. This is because if the different kind of machines and tools which are based on different kind of sophisticated technology. With this advancement, sewing has become the passion for a number of people around the globe. We have written this book, keeping in mind the interest if a number of our readers.

Thank you for downloading *"Sewing for beginners-A complete guide for learning the sewing techniques"*. All over the book, the different chapters have been allocated to the different issues pertaining to sewing and stitching. All the topics covered in the book are truly meant for helping our readers in establishing a firm practice about the art of sewing. So you need to give a look to all these chapters so that any critical chapter cannot be overlooked.

But the account straight away extends the speed throughout the subsequent chapters. The basis of starting with the preface information is very logical. It is projected to make up all of the readers exclusively recognizable with the meditation of the topic.

The book starts with a brief but elaborative note about the basic concepts of sewing. So all you need is to first grab all these concepts and then move on to learning the practical features. The concepts are mentioned in a way which will be beneficial to apply in the practical aspect of sewing. The discussion then extends to the sewing tools and devices, so that the reader can easily apply the concepts in judging the right type of tool. All the types of techniques are elaborately discussed so that the readers can easily choose the appropriate technique, according to the type of the fabric and the pattern to be made. We hope that we have become successful in elaborating all the important issues to our readers, so that the manuscript can serve as the complete guide to the sewing practice.

Chapter 1:
The equipment and devices needed in Sewing

It is rightly said that the tools make the art more obvious. It means that whatever art or activity you are going to perform you need to be equipped with all the essential tools and devices. Sometimes a person is very much skilled and possesses all the competencies, yet there are certain restrictions due to non-working devices and equipment which make it really impossible for the person to show his talent.

Sewing is a totally machine driven activity. It demands from the sewing person that all the devices are checked for the perfect working so that all of the sewing activities run smoothly and without any error. Below are some of the equipment which you will need, if you are interested in learning the art of sewing.

- Sewing machine

- Cardboard measuring mat

- Iron and small ironing boards that work on any flat surface)

- Sewing machine

- Sharp scissors, if possible, used only for sewing

- Measuring tape (the soft and the flexible one works best)

- Sturdy thread (very light thread is easy to break and it jam your machine)

- Seam ripper (an absolute *must* for removing stray stitches and icky seams)

- Straight pins, small to medium sized

Sewing machine and its basics

The sewing machine lies at the heart of sewing. So as a learner you need to know all about this basic tool which will help you in making your sewing more compatible and perfect.

The basic parts of a sewing machine include the following:

1. Power Switch

The power switch may have variable alignment, depending upon the model of the machine. Mostly the power switch is the connection of power supply to the machine, which can run the machine in or off. Mostly the power and the light switches are separate. If there are children surrounding the areas, where the machine is placed, it is a good option to keep the switch off, to allow greater safety. If the machine is without power switch, the safety protocols can be enhanced using the safety strip, which is connected to the main power supply.

2. Light

Good light access is indispensable for successful sewing. The location of the light varies with the model of the machine. Some machines have more than one light location. But the light at the needle area and pressure foot is highly essential. Light may be connected to the power supply or sometimes it is without it, operated with battery supply.

3. Stitches

Every sewing machine has variable number of stitches which are to be selected, as and when needed. So the selection of the appropriate stitch is very essential. There are variable stitches; straight stitches are for seaming of traditional style, whereas the decorative stitches help in different kind of pattern making. Selecting the right stitch for the right type of dress makes your stitching outclass. The major basics include blind hem, straight,

Zigzag, buttonhole and mending stitches are the major types. There reverse stitching can be used to anchor the seams. As the basic knowledge you need to know about width capabilities and stitch length.

For creative decorative possibilities, many machines present a myriad of decorative stitches. But have a large type of stitches, cannot guarantee the effectiveness of your machine. If you are a learner you can start with the most basic stitches, even if fewer.

4. Display Screen

The recent models of digital sewing machines have an LCD or LED display screen, form which one can choose the tension adjustments and the stitch options. The art of producing a good stitch lies in balancing the thread tension between the Upper and lower thread. Some digital machines have the option of numbering the external dials for the alterations of the upper tension. In manual machines it needs to be adjusted by hand. In case of the bobbin thread, the tension is amendable with a screw on the bobbin casing.

5. Presser Feet

First of all you need to know that how many presser feet come with your machine model. The basic types of presser feet include:

- A multipurpose foot is made to stitch straight and zigzag stitches for basic sewing

- Zipper foot,

- Buttonhole foot

- Blind hem foot

- Teflon foot for sticky fabrics,

- Decorative stitch feet

- Narrow hemming feet

- And hundreds more depending on the machine model

There are different categories of presser feet. These include the brand-specific Feet, which are available only from a dealer and the generic feet, which you can get from the notion companies or the fabric store. You can easily handle both of these feet on your machine, provided you are well aware of the purpose of the feet.

Many machines give the option to alter the pressure on any type of the presser foot, so that any fabric, whether thick or thin can easily be adjusted, for both thick and thin fabric.

Some Machines also possess extra lifting space so that you can easily insert thick fabrics.

6. Thread Delivery

One of the critical tools of the sewing machines is the spool pins, which are used to hold the thread. Sewing machines have multiple numbers of vertical and horizontal spools. Novelty and metallic threads often entail rotate positioning to nourish properly without tangling, binding or slipping. If your sewing machine possesses more than one spool pin, it can then allow you to use more than one needle, so that different decorative patterns can be made. This information is usually provided in the manuals of the sewing machines.

7. Bobbins

The sewing machine possesses bobbins, which are the main source if forming the stitches. Some machines possess the option to win the bobbin, while others may lack this option. The level of thread in the bobbin may be detected by the built in sensors. These sensors allow you to know when the bobbin is low in thread. Likewise when the bobbin is full the sensor will let you know. These sensors allow smooth stitching, so that stitching is not interrupted due to lack of thread.

8. Needle Position

Computerized and digital sewing machine models have the option for the adjustment of multiple needle positions. This is imperative if you desire to rotate your stitching line to the different directions while keeping the fabric on the full width. You need to learn how to fix the needle position, according to the varying width of the fabric.

Chapter 2:
The basic sewing techniques

Now when we have made our way a little easy by discussing the major concepts of sewing and the related devices and tools, we can easily direct our attention towards the major sewing techniques. The techniques discussed here are mostly the most frequently used techniques of sewing.

Essential basics of sewing

- As the basic rule of sewing, you will stitch the *right side* of the fabric together. Right side is the one which is the finished side of the dress or other accessory. As a general guideline the right side is usually brighter and shiner. When you will be using this rule, the untidy look of the stitches, will not be showed and the dress or any other item, you are sewing will give a neat look

- The seam allowance refers to distance between stitch and the edge of the fabric. As a regular rule this distance is usually ¼ inches. But it is not a rule of thumb, the critical factor is that whatever seam allowance you choose for your stitching, it needs to be well estimated before, so that you can cut that approximated length extra for your fabric. It means that seam allowance will let you cut your cloth to an appropriate length.

Begin your stitching

We will begin with the illustrations of straight seams:

1. Start with straight seam and for this you need to have your fabric or cloth and fold it to the right sides.

2. Place put in the machine in a way that the presser foot and unfolded edges are in line with each other. It will help you to get an accurate seam allowance.

3. Now turn the wheel of your machine in such a way, that it is towards the lower needle and then into the scrap.

4. The next comes the presser foot. Put it down, with the help of the lever provided at its back. Make sure that whenever you start sewing the presser feet is down. It will allow you to have a smooth and steady sewing and the cloth will be automatically into the machine. You just need a slight guidance in the form of adjusting the fabric.

5. The next step is to press the foot pedal so that you can stitch forward.

6. The reverse button of your machine will help you stitch a few stitches backwards. In this case you will not need to tie a knot at the end of your stitch and your seam will remain locked and safe.

7. Keep stitching forward until you reach to the outer end of the cloth. Then repeat the process of backward stitching and then stitch forward. During this process, you have to keep the needle to its highest position so that the needle cannot get unthreaded.

8. Once you are done with the forward and the backward stitching of the fabric, remove it from the machine and make it off from the machine. For this you will need to raise the presser feet.   When you remove the fabric make sure that you cut all the unnecessary thread form the end of the fabric in this way these extra threads will not come in the way of your subsequent sewing.

Now turn your cloth towards the right side and enjoy your beautiful seam. If any way you find that you cannot get your seam, the way you want, keep your seam ripper handy, so that you can easily do what you want.

Sewing up And Down the Corners

When you are sewing any kind of dress or even if you are stitching some other accessory, you may not always get the same straight seam. And if this had been the case, it had become extremely difficult and time consuming. So now we will move to make the sewing instructions forward, towards the corners.

1. You have to adjust the seam allowance yourself. Within this seam allowance when you come across a turn, you need to fix the needle into the fabric and side by side you have to raise the presser feet.

2. You will hang the fabric into the left side and the lowered needle will keep your fabric fixed.

3. Now adjust the presser feet of the machine in a way so that you can continue sewing with the adjusted fabric and sewing machine.

The Rounding Curves

You will need to curve the rounding corners just the way we have discussed above in the corner section. When you will round the corners, you may use just the tilted hand movements, which will be enough for you to make the adjusted movements. For more tilted corners you will need to pivot your fabric and then move along the needle.

Whenever your fabric becomes hard to steer, keep yourself slow and see if the fabric is adjusted. If not you may then lower your needle and raise the presser foot alongside. You may need to repeat this movement time and again so that your fabric gets adjusted normally.

In case of the curved seams we suggest you that you snip your seam allowance from different consecutive places so that the dress will be easy to turn to right side. But one thing for which you need to be cautious is to make the snips very carefully. On your way towards, snipping the edges you may cut your seam. So make your snip carefully and professionally.

Chapter 3:
The special techniques of Sewing

In the last section we have made an effort for all the beginners that they can easily understand the basics of seaming and stitching. But for a learner, this is not enough. One needs to move forward for enhancing towards the special techniques of sewing and stitching.

Hemming

Hemming is needed at the end of the trousers, necklines and at the end of sleeves. Moreover the raveling of fabric can be avoided by making beautiful hemming. Following are the major steps of hemming:

1. Turn around your fabric to an appropriate seam allowance. In most of the cases a turn of ¼ inch will be enough. Now when you have turned the edge equally you need to press the fabric over the turn. It will give the fabric, a settled and pressed look.

2. Pin up the folded portion in a way that the fabric gets settled in your hand. Moreover, if you will add too much pins, it will eventually disturb you in sewing, so you need to make an accurate adjustment in this regard. Now stitch at the pressed folds.

3. There may be cases when you will need softer hems. In all these instances, you will make your hem through the hand using a needle and the thread.

Use two threads for creating a gathering

Gathering technique in sewing is basically used for all those accessories and dresses which need a little ruffle. It creates marvelous fullness in skirts, sleeves and hats. But gathering technique to be applied needs some extra fabric, so it is necessary that if your plan is to go for the gathering you must plan it ahead, so that you are equipped with all the necessary items and fabrics, well before time. Gathering can be either light or intense and in both these cases the quantity of fabric needed, will vary.

In gathering technique the first step is to have a correct seam allowance. One thing which people usually forget is a double seam allowance. As there will be a double seam for gathering so, you need to keep your seam allowance double than the normal.

Another technique used in the gathering is the known as basting. For that you need to need to keep your stitch length, as long as possible.

Now make the first seam along the length of the cloth at a width of ¼ inches. Now when you are completed with first seam, make another seam at a distance of ¼ inches. Now you will get two consecutive seams. But be careful do not cut off the threads at the end of each seam. These threads will be used to create the gathers.

Now when done with seams, gently pull off the threads from one end, by keeping a hand on the other. Gentle pulling will enable gathering to be created. Now adjust the gathering in such a way that the gathers are adjusted evenly on the fabric.

Another technique is to pull the threads from both the ends, so that you can get more saturated gathers.

Appliqué work

This is a very beautiful pattern making technique, which can add decorative ability of your dress or any other accessory.

1. Cut the shape of the cloth into different designs. These will be the designs appearing as the pattern on another cloth. So cut the shape very finely.

2. Now you will put the cut piece on the fabric, on which you want to paste the desired shape. Market is full of different products which can help you to enhance the ability of the cut piece to get sticker to the fabric. One such product is called fusible web.

3. Use a zigzag stitch in order to keep it firm, cut the pattern on place. Stitch around the corners, alongside the edges, so that the shape cannot get distorted. One trick here is to keep the zigzag stitch only on the piece placed on the fabric. Do not stitch your underneath fabric along.

French seam

French seams are also another beautiful style for making your dress extremely decorative and stylish. French seam will prevent any kind of ravel of the fabric so you can easily prevent raveling by just a simple trick of French seaming.

1. First of all, turn your fabric to the wrong side and stitch it to the end.

2. Now turn it to the right side and make another stitch till the end of the fabric. Make sure that the second seam is apart from the first seam and it makes use of the distance left between.

These were a few of the sewing techniques which are largely used in a number of different sewing techniques. Although these have been provided with a step by step approach, yet you can also make your own innovative styles by hit and trial method.

Chapter 4:
Some Sewing Tutorials- easy to follow

In this chapter apart from some basic tutorials which will serve as the basic guide to all those who want to practice sewing at home.

Sewing on a button:

The reason for explaining button sewing is its frequent need in all household routines. Sometimes just hanging a button needs for someone's help, so here we want to make our readers get familiar with this simple task. Knowing the simpler things first is more crucial than starting the harder ones.

In the market, you can find, two major types of buttons.

Flat buttons have a body of the button with a whole, from where the thread is directly administrated to attach the button.

Shank buttons are slightly different, in a way that they possess a tiny eyelet like opening, which ultimately extends to the back of the button. The back opens up into a hole, which serves the purpose of attaching the button. These holes extends from the back of the button with a hole for attaching the button. The shank buttons are usually used more for the decorative purposes, as the upper side of shank buttons can easily fulfill the purpose of decoration.

Sewing:

1. Cut a thread of about 24" length.

2. Put thread in the needle and form a loop of the thread in a way that thread is folded on itself.

3. Catching both ends of the thread place a knot at the end so that you will work with double thread. It will add strength to your button. Trim the extended thread

4. Mark the location over the fabric where you exactly want to place the button. Through that marking pull the needle up.

5. Make a Stitch in the shape of "X" on that location

6. Placing the stitched "X" as you steer, bring the needle through one hole of the needle, when the button is slightly raised from the fabric surface. Make the stitch diagonally across it, until the four holes are stitched completely. Sometimes you may get a two holes button. In that case, stitching will be based on just two holes.

7. Bring your needle and thread from side to side along the fabric once more, but this time it will be under the button.

8. Wrap the thread tightly along the base of the button and of you are unsure to be light, make it three to four times. Make a loop and trim the extended thread.

In order to sew a shank button, the basic steps will be the same and only few slight alterations will be needed. As there is a shank already, so you need not to place a space between the fabric and the button. Moreover, while stitching through the holes, you will only stitch through the shank, as the shank is serving as the hole. So you will not sew over and over again, as you did in case of flat button.

Pockets stitching

If you are interested in sewing, you will encounter majorly two types of pockets.

1. Side seam Pocket

2. Shirt Pocket

Sewing the Side Seam Pocket

1. Add the extensions on the sides of the frock or skirt. Extension serves as the facings of the pocket. The measurement should be about 2"more than the hand that will be using the pocket.

2. Draw the pockets in the desired shape.

3. Mark with a pencil and Stitch on each side of the corners of the facings. Clip from the edge and stitch must not be cut. Make a stitching box along the facing so that the thread will reinforce its strength.

4. Now make the stitch on the pocket, in such a way that the right side of the pocket is attached to the wrong side of the skirt or shirt. Stitching must be done along the curved edges.

5. Now you will stitch the skirt or shirt on which you are placing the pocket. Place the stitches from the front of the skirt to its back along the side seam. In this step be careful that you do not sew the pocket edge, edge it will be sewed into the seam. Press firmly to give a neat look.

Sewing the Shirt Pocket

1. Cut the pocket piece in a rectangular piece. The pocket size you want finally must be marked and additional allowance for 1/2" for upper hem and seam allowances on the other three sides.

2. Press the three lower edges with the help of an iron. Also press under the hem.

3. Turn the pocket to its right side. Make a Topstitch upper hem into place

4. Place the pocket on the skirt or shirt front. Make sure that the pocket is right side up.

5. Stitch into the shirt roughly around the lower three sides. The fourth side, that will be the top side, will be left open. Strengthen the corners of the shirt pocket with the help of stitching.

Chapter 5:
Some Important Issues Pertaining To Sewing

This all discussion, brings us to the end of this book. Throughout the book we have kept our focus towards making our text simple and easily readable and understandable for all those who are new to this field of sewing. Sewing is not that hard, if you make it your passion. Like all other forms of art it also demands practice and lots of involvement. So if you also want to make your sewing practice brilliant, try to create a passion for it. Step by step approach is always best to get to the highest level.

Below are some of the important issues discussed for our readers, which may not be direct sewing techniques. Yet keeping in mind all of these will eventually aid your sewing technique.

Pressing also comes under the sewing issues. For most of the commercial sewing centers, pressing is given a lot of importance. Pressing the ready dress or other accessory can eventually change the look of your dress. Ironing should be done in a step by step way, such that every seam is pressed after done. It will give a neater look to your costume.

Selecting the right type of fabric and then using the right type of sewing technique is very much crucial. As the sewing and clothing industry has flourished a lot of new and artificial fabric are now also a part of the sewing and clothing industry. So if your fabric is stretchable or is very thin you need to choose the sewing machine very efficiently. Moreover, pressing the stretchable and thin fabric is also very tricky. Keeping the heat very low will make it untidy and using it too high can make the fabric burn so you need to make an appropriate choice according to the type of the fabric.

Sewing is also an art, so you need to make your art flourish using the appropriate equipment and the accessories. The electronic accessory market is full of new innovations. But one thing which all the learners must know is the importance of learning the manual sewing. Although sewing is much easier and technology based now yet until you know the basics of real sewing, you cannot use these technology based solutions of sewing patterns. So get yourself equipped, both with the skills and the appropriate devices, which can have your way towards easy and neat sewing.

This brings us to the end of this short discussion about the different sewing patterns and techniques. This topic is so wide and diverse that we can even write dozens of books on the topic of sewing. We have tried to make our discussion comprehensive yet elaborative. We want to help our readers in making their sewing brilliant and full of effectiveness. You can easily use these basic techniques of sewing and make them improved, by practicing again and again. The major devices and tools used in swing will help you in one way or the other.

Conclusion

Coming to the end of the book, I want to make my readers greet about having such a useful manuscript, which can not only bring their talent out, but also make their art of sewing more polished and elaborate. I think we have been successful in the aim of making our readers fully guided about starting their basic practice of sewing. One thing I would like to mention in the end is the need of continuous practicing. We have mentioned all the techniques with a step by step approach, but what we expect from the readers is to make use of this knowledge to the fullest extent.

We have followed a step by step approach so that it can help the beginners to get an easy way for their sewing practice. The basics devices and tools are also mentioned so that our readers can choose the most appropriate tool for the different type of fabric and pattern. We wish that our readers can get well versed in all their sewing ventures. If you enjoyed this book, please be kind and leave a review for this book on Amazon.